Exploring a Theme: Worship

Helping children gain an awareness of the importance of worship in the lives of people, individually and in the community, extends children's knowledge and understanding of the world around them and also provides an opportunity for their own spiritual development through reflection on the spirituality of others.

In this book we offer some practical, active and visual learning strategies to help children enjoy learning about and learning from worship.

One important way of helping pupils 'encounter' religion is through 'meeting' people from faiths and 'hearing' their 'story'. Encounter with real-life visitors is often the best learning experience, but when this is not possible a good alternative is the use of resources in which individuals talk about their own experiences and beliefs.

To find out more about how and why people worship today we asked children from four main faith traditions in Britain to share their thoughts with us. These interviews start on on page 16 and are also on the RE Today website. Here children speak about their experience of worship, not as representatives of their faiths, but as individuals. Their insights provide a fascinating glimpse into the personal significance of worship, as understood by them, at a particular moment of time.

We have chosen to focus on the four religions most commonly explored in primary RE. By interviewing at least two people from each, we aim to give a flavour of the different forms of expression worship can take within and between religions today. The approach can be applied to other religions and beliefs in your local area. The activities provided with each interview aim to help you make the most of these 'insights', to engage your pupils with the key experiences and beliefs identified.

Joyce Mackley
Editor

RE Today weblink:

www.retoday.org.uk

The RE Today website provides some additional resources and classroom-ready materials for subscribers. Look out for the 'RE Today on the web' logo at the end of selected articles. The password for access can be found in each term's *REtoday* magazine.

Contents

Singing, miming, sharing – exploring worship with younger children

4-6

For the teacher

This unit suggests three fun, child-friendly activities to get younger pupils talking and thinking about some of the things people do when they 'worship'.

Worship is central to the lives of millions of people. Some children will belong to religious families with experience of worship: others will only encounter it through school assembly and visits to local places of worship. Providing young children with opportunities to understand that people have different beliefs and cultures is an important way of fostering their own spiritual development and encouraging the development of respect and understanding for their family's beliefs and those of others.

The activities in the following pages are:

1. **Singing praises!** Using a child-friendly Christian praise song to spark children's creativity and stimulate their imagination to make up their own song of praise!

2. **Miming a prayer:** Devising a mime to represent the ideas in a prayer and to think about the sorts of things people talk to God about. This provides an opportunity for talking about what children think God is like and why people might tell him their most secret and wonderful thoughts.

3. **Sharing with others:** Another form worship takes is in action, in service to others. A good focus here is food – the sharing of food in worship and the sharing of food in the world. This tasting and talking activity links to the sharing of food during worship such as

   • bread and wine (Christian)

   • challah bread (Judaism)

   • prashad (Hinduism and Sikhism)

   and to how people show their love for God by caring for other people.

What is worship?

• The word derives from 'worth-ship': to do with what is of highest worth; responding to this with devotion and honour.

• Worship has many forms of expression, varying from one tradition to another and within any given act of worship.

• Forms of expression include words spoken and sung; readings from sacred texts; rituals and movement; silence; prayer; sharing of symbolic food and practical service.

Links to Early Learning goals

The activities outlined here contribute to the development of:

• **Language for communication:** listening with enjoyment and responding to stories, songs and other music.

• **Sense of community:** – understanding that people have different cultures and beliefs that need to be treated with respect.

I can ...

The following pupil-friendly criteria could be used to assess children's responses to the activities. Level 1 describes what most 6-year-olds should be able to do.

Level 1

• use **religious words and phrases** to recognise and name some things people do when they worship

• **talk about** some feelings associated with worship (such as being peaceful; joyful; thankful) and their own experience of these.

Singing praises

For the teacher/ practitioner

People praise God in a variety of ways – singing; gestures; actions. The following activity uses all three!

Activity:

- **Play a lively 'praise' song** for children to listen to. Christian gospel choir music is a good source. Encourage children to **move or clap in time to the music**. Notice how gospel choirs don't stand still when they are singing! Why is this? How does the music make them feel?

- Explain to the children that you are going to think about times when people are really happy and how people often want to praise and say thank you to God for the good things they enjoy.

- **Think/pair/share** Ask children to think for themselves about 'Happy times'. Share their ideas with a partner. Each pair feeds back ideas to the group. Display ideas. Make the focus being thankful for 'happy times'.

- **Tell the story** about Jesus healing the lame man (Luke Ch 17 v11-19) and how he said 'Thank you, Lord'. A lovely version of this story called 'The Man who Came Back' can be found in *The Lion Storyteller Bible* by Bob Hartman (paperback ISBN 978-07459-3607 9).

  ° What was he thankful for?
  ° What song might he have sung?

- Have a go at **creating a simple song**, or find and sing a praise song from your school collective worship resources. **'Praise ye the Lord, Alleluia'** is a simple repetitive song all children could take part in. Make this an **action song** by getting half the group to sing Alleluia and half to sing 'praise ye the Lord'. Each group stands when their word or phrase is sung – so lots of standing and sitting – and lots of careful listening! You can find this song and activity on the *Praise God with Sticky Kids* CD (see resource list).

Praise Ye the Lord

Allelu, allelu, allelu, alleluia, praise ye the Lord

Allelu, allelu, allelu, alleluia, praise ye the Lord

Praise ye the Lord, alleluia

Praise ye the Lord, alleluia

Praise ye the Lord, alleluia

Praise ye the Lord.

Traditional

Some useful resources

For child-friendly praise and worship songs from Christianity, Judaism and Islam see for example:

Christianity:

The following CDs, made for worship, can be used as resources in RE when linked to appropriate activities:

Praise God with the Sticky Kids www.stickykids.net. Favourite Bible stories with songs, rhymes and riddles about caring and sharing in the world. Aimed at the under 5s.

Come and Praise songs for collective worship from the BBC are used in many schools. These are drawn from the Christian tradition but with inclusive content.

Judaism:

Two Candles Burn by Stephen Melzack. Ten songs capture the essence of Jewish worship and festivals for children in the 4–11 age group. Available from the RE Today catalogue: www.retoday.org.uk.

Islam:

Children of Heaven by Zain Bhikha. A compilation of 15 songs for young children written and sung by Zain Bhikha, a well-known Muslim nasheed artist. Available from the RE Today catalogue (see above).

Miming a prayer

4–6

For the teacher/ practitioner

Prayer is a worship activity in all religions. Here we use mime to represent the ideas expressed in the most famous Christian prayer – The Lord's Prayer – and to think about what people talk to God about. The approach can be applied to age-appropriate prayers for any religion.

The process of working out the mime focuses the attention of the pupil, requires empathy and reflection, and helps to raise awareness of the power of inner feelings.

Pupils, working in pairs or small groups, devise a mime to represent the outward expression of an inner feeling (joy, sympathy) or key idea (forgiveness, God) expressed in the words of the prayer. Feelings are expressed through movement of the body and expressions on the face.

For younger children, suggest that they follow your lead to start off with – but feel free to improvise their own actions. Make the movements slightly larger than life.

Follow-on activities

1. Looking at children's prayers: a guessing game

Collect some simple children's prayers. Copy them on to cards, enough for everyone to have a good choice. Ask children to pick a prayer they like.

In pairs children **talk about** how the person who said the prayer is feeling. Ask them to make up a mime to show others the way the person feels.

Children **perform their mimes** and other children guess what feeling the prayer is telling God about. The performers then read out the prayer to the others. Did they guess correctly?

Make a list of the feelings in the prayers.

Explain that prayer is talking to God. People can tell God anything. **Pose a question** 'I wonder what God is like? What do you think? Suggest some ideas, for example 'God is like a massive computer taking lots of messages all the time!' 'God is like my mum – everyone takes their problems to her!'

2. Paper chain

Pupils could **make a prayer chain** by writing their own thoughts or prayers on small lengths of sticky-backed paper which are then made into loops and joined together to form a chain, which can be displayed.

A focus from the Lord's Prayer might be 'saying sorry', 'God's world' or 'a good world' – with children writing about what they think would make the world a happy place that God would be pleased with.

Miming the Lord's Prayer (Matthew 6: 7–13)

Our father in heaven [*All raise arms and look upwards*]

Hallowed be your name [*extending arms outwards, bowing down in honour*]

Your kingdom come [*arms spread wide, turning round slowly*]

Your will be done, on earth as it is in heaven [*joining hands; smiling; lifting arms to show joy/happiness*]

Give us this day our daily bread [*eating movements; rubbing tummy/smiling*]

And forgive us when we do wrong [*arms to chest; facial expression showing sorry*]

As we forgive those who hurt us [*arms spread wide; friendly welcoming facial expression*]

And do not lead us into temptation [*serious face, shaking head, gestures saying no*]

But keep us away from bad things [*turn around to show your back*]

For yours is the kingdom, the power and the glory, for ever and ever. Amen

[*hands together and bow heads briefly to end*]

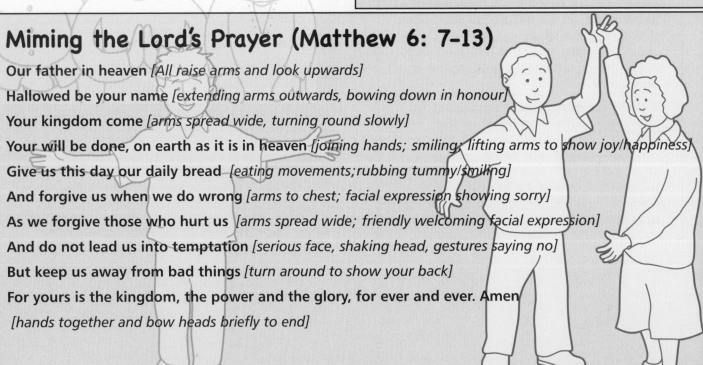

Sharing with others....

For the teacher/ practitioner

Another form worship takes is in action, in service to others. A good focus here is food – the sharing of food in worship and the sharing of food in the world. This tasting and talking activity links to the sharing of food during worship such as

- bread and wine (Christian)
- challah bread or Sukkoth (Judaism)
- prashad in Hinduism and Sikhism

and to how people show they love God by caring for other people.

Information file

Food plays an important role in religion.

- Foods are associated with religious festivals and holy days: for example, hot cross buns for Christians at Easter, potato latkes for Jews at Hanukkah, challah loaves and wine at Shabbat.

- Food plays an important part in religious worship rituals and ceremonies: for example, karah prasad, a specially cooked sweet pudding blessed through prayer in the presence of the Guru Granth Sahib and then distributed to all worshippers, demonstrating the two key Sikh values – sewa (service) and equality; bread and wine shared during holy communion, Eucharist or Lord's Supper in Christianity.

- Dietary laws often reflect beliefs about creation and about humanity's relationship with the created world, with each other and with God. Kashrut (kosher) dietary laws are kept by many Orthodox Jews; halal food laws determine what is lawful or permitted in Islam; many Hindus are vegetarian in respect of beliefs about ahimsa (non-violence).

Some starting points for the classroom

- Exploring **Hanukkah** with younger children – taste potato latkes and talk about why food cooked in oil is a good way of remembering the story of Hanukkah.

- Exploring **Easter** with younger children – ask them to look closely at a hot cross bun. What do they see on it? What might it mean? When do people traditionally eat these?

- Exploring **Sikhism** – make and taste some karah prasad and explore the significance of giving, receiving and sharing food as a sign of welcome and equality.

- **Make a class or school cookbook** including favourite recipes from a range of religions. This could then be sold as a fundraising exercise and the proceeds given to a charity which is seeking to alleviate hunger in the world.

A recipe for karah prasad

Karah prasad is shared by worshippers and visitors in a gurdwara – a Sikh place of worship. It is eaten with the fingers. Worshippers receive it into open hands as a symbol of receiving, as opposed to taking, God's gifts.

100g unsalted butter

50g plain flour

100g semolina or ground rice

100g sugar and 425ml water boiled together

1. Melt the butter in a saucepan and add the flour, beating well with a wooden spoon over a very gentle heat.

2. Add the semolina or ground rice, continuing to beat well.

3. Heat until the butter separates

4. Remove from the heat and add the sugared water very gradually, stirring until a stiff paste has formed.

5. Cool slightly before eating.

Exploring Christmas and Easter through children's eyes

5–7

For the teacher

These learning ideas for 5–7s approach the two most significant Christian festivals through the experience of two children. This is a good method, enabling learners to make links to their own lives more easily than if they hear about religion only from adults. This work assumes that children have heard the Christmas and Easter stories of Jesus.

Copy the next page of quotes from Rebekah and Sam about their church and what happens there at Christmas and Easter. These two children also feature on pages 18 and 19 of this publication, and on the RE Today website supplementary materials for subscribers, talking about worship.

Activity 1 Read together and quiz

Ask two able readers in the group to be 'Sam' and 'Rebekah'. Have them read out the quotations one by one to the class, in turn. Then ask the children these questions (make it a team quiz if you like):

1. What was Sam's Christmas play called?

2. What fruit is a Christingle made from?

3. Why does a Christingle have a candle in it?

4. What is Rebekah's favourite thing about Christingles?

5. Where was Jesus born in the Christmas story?

6. What food did Sam make for Easter?

7. What does the bread and wine stand for in Christian worship?

8. What unusual thing did Sam and Rebekah have in their church at Easter?

9. How many thieves were in the Easter play?

10. Why did Rebekah think God was pleased with the Bouncy Castle?

Activity 2 Who's most important in the Christmas story?

Use the little drawings here, blown up if you like, or the PowerPoint presentation for subscribers on the RE Today website (get the password from this term's *REtoday* magazine).

- Put the figures on the floor, and identify them all to the pupils. Tell them that all these characters are going to be in the Christmas play, until people start getting poorly on the morning of the play.

- Which character could they do without?

- Do they really need three shepherds?

Invite a volunteer to take away one character and give a reason. And another. And another.

When there are just two left (Mary and Jesus perhaps?) discuss with the class why they are the most important in the story. Do the same activity for the Easter story.

Activity 3 Speculating; guessing; hot-seating

Ask the children to pair and share their ideas about what **questions** they might ask Sam and Rebekah about their church and about Christmas and Easter. They might write them down. Then have two children take the roles of Sam and Rebekah and try to answer the questions the rest of the class have come up with.

Celebrating Christmas and Easter at church

Sam (8) and Rebekah (10) live in Leicester with their mum and dad. They are members of Holy Trinity Church, which is an Anglican church.

'The Christmas service at Holy Trinity Church is brilliant. There is always a play with grownups and children in it. Last year it was called "The Grumpy Innkeeper" and it was really funny.'

Sam

'At the Christmas service, we all were given a Christingle. It's made of an orange, that is like the world, and a red ribbon around it as a reminder of when Jesus died, and a candle in the top of it, because Jesus is the light of the world. Then there are four lots of sweets on little sticks in the orange, for the four corners of the earth. We like the sweets best.'

Rebekah

'I like the Easter Extravaganza as well. We have a special event for children at Easter. We made special Easter biscuits, and there is really good music, with another play that tells the story of Jesus dying and coming back to life. It was about two thieves in Jerusalem, and it was funny. It was shocking too!'

Sam

'Our church has a really big main room, and on Sundays it is set out with chairs for hundreds of people, but at the Easter Extravaganza, we cleared all the chairs away and we had a bouncy castle, right inside the church.'

Rebekah

'My favourite thing in Explorers at church was when we made scenes from stories in the Bible, it was fun. We had a big Christmas party too, and our leaders got custard pies.'

Sam

'I don't think God minds this. I think God likes to see the children happy and bouncing in church, and it might make more children come along, like some of my friends from school have done.'

Rebekah

'I think about the story of Jesus, when he broke the bread and shared the wine with his disciples and he said that the bread stands for his body and the wine stands for his blood.'

Sam

'We had a special competition to make a nativity scene one year. But we had to imagine that it was Jesus being born in the modern world, not in Bethlehem. I made a model of mine, and got second prize. My friend Anna won.'

Rebekah

Activities to try: You could...

(a) Make a nativity scene where baby Jesus is born in your town. Use Lego® or Playmobil® or make a cardboard model. What would it be like if this story happened today?

(b) Look at a Christingle, and find out more about the symbols Rebekah talks about.

(c) Make some Easter biscuits. Decorate them with some symbols for Jesus from the story such as cross, palm leaf, light, bread and wine.

(d) 'Alive again'. Christians believe that when Jesus died, after three days he came alive again. Read simple versions of the stories from Luke ch.24.

© 2009 RE Today Services
Permission is granted to photocopy this page for use in classroom activities in schools that have purchased this publication.

What do we worship? 7-9

For the teacher

Here are some RE activities for pupils that explore these questions:

- What matters more than money?
- What do we worship? Is it what is most precious?
- Is worship what we do to show what really matters most?

These practical teaching ideas aim to help children to notice the values of material things, and of spiritual things, and to think for themselves about what they value. The learning draws on Christianity, Buddhism and Islam.

The **learning objectives** for the unit are to enable pupils to:

- **understand** some teaching from Christianity, Buddhism and Islam about material possessions and about some things that are more valuable, that 'money can't buy'
- **reflect** upon some of the things that money can't buy, and their value and importance for human happiness and well-being.

Worth much more than money: some ideas from 7 year olds

people	a heart
love	the moon
happiness	a friend
your dad	the stars
hugs and kisses	thunder
rain	earwax
the life of a tree	the world
the air	

Classroom activities

1. What matters more than money?

We asked some 7-year-old pupils about the things that matter the most. The process is outlined below. Try it with your class and see what they come up with.

- Begin with two minutes in silence, looking at a bowl full of money (ours looked like a thousand pounds, but it wasn't real! Use some copies of one side of a note coloured in).
- Ask pupils to think about the things they could do with the money if it was theirs, or other thoughts that occur to them.
- Now place an empty bowl in front of the class with a title *'worth much more than money'*. Spend two minutes silently looking at the empty bowl. In groups of three, ask pupils to make a list of things that money can't buy. (Below is a list of some of the things ours suggested.)
- Talk about why these things are precious. Discuss whether some of the things money can't buy are priceless.

2. What does it mean to say that something is 'priceless'?

- In circle time, go round with the prompt 'I would not ever swap or sell…'. Make a list of all the things children think are worth more than money.
- Show the children a special object such as a wedding ring. Talk about: This ring might cost £100, but is that all it's worth? What else can they think of that's like it, worth more than money?
- Use a feely bag, or blindfolds to explore some religious artefacts from several different faiths, or give children in groups a religious artefact (such as those chosen by the children in the interviews on pages 16–33). Ask children to draw, describe, label and think about the object. Talk about the difference between 'what it cost in the shops' and 'what it's worth to a believer'.
- Put a 'price tag' on each artefact to show how much it might cost to buy.
- Ask children to decide what it might be worth to a believer. Our answers included 'lots and lots' (of a figurine of the Madonna), 'it is special to Sikh people' (of a kara). The children had learned a simple thing from religion: that cash value is not the only value.

3. Who worships what?

Here is a guessing game. Read each card out to the class and ask them to answer the question.....

WHO OR WHAT DOES THIS PERSON WORSHIP?

She looks in the mirror all the time.

Her favourite book is her own diary.

She is writing her autobiography

She spends money on designer clothes, hair gel, bags and shoes.

She is happiest when people praise her.

If people don't do it – she praises herself!

He is always reading 'Argos' and 'Toys R Us' catalogues.

He tries to buy the 'top ten toys' each year.

He gets angry if anyone touches his toys and doesn't want to share them.

His favourite day is his birthday, but he has a really short party for lots of people to come to. That way he gets lots of presents but doesn't have to share them for long.

He calls Saturday 'Toy Day' every week.

He goes to church every Sunday.

He likes to read the Bible.

He tries to be really kind to his family and friends, and to say his prayers.

He likes singing and dancing to praise God.

His favourite day of the year is Easter, and his second favourite is Christmas.

She watches TV all the time.

She goes to the TV studios for her holidays and likes to tour the sets of all the soaps.

She reads *TV Times* and *Radio Times* in bed. She has spent all her money on a 50-inch plasma screen, so she is very hungry.

Her eyes are square.

Her favourite time of the year is Christmas, because the telly is better then.

Her nightmare is the aerial or the satellite dish getting blown off the roof.

She loves to pray five times a day, and she never misses one.

Her favourite book is the Qur'an. She keeps it wrapped and on a high shelf.

She enjoys giving £1 away every time she gets £40.

Her ambition is to visit Mecca in Saudi Arabia.

Her favourite place in town is the mosque and she always remembers to fast during Ramadan.

He likes to visit the bank a lot.

He buys a newspaper called the *Financial Times*.

He thinks the worst day of the year is a bank holiday, and he has a big wallet.

His favourite place is the Royal Mint

He never gives 10p to charity or to a homeless person.

His greatest fear is being 'skint'.

He has short arms and deep pockets.

Follow-on activities

1. In pairs, ask children to write another 'worshippers paragraph' like these for a person who worships football; a Ferrari; food; a pet; or a pop band. Use the thinking frame activity on page 10 to start this off.

2. Draw out the learning carefully to show that religious worship is in some ways more serious, more long-lived and more widespread than the 'silly' worship of some of these examples.

3. Ask pupils to work out a definition of worship with examples.

4. Pupils might reflect on what they worship, and how worship affects their own behaviour. They can use the same thinking frame for this.

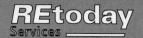
4. 'What matters most to you is what you worship.' An activity to get children thinking

- Put up five large sheets of paper around the room with headings and appropriate photographs for: football; Ferrari; food; pets; pop band.

- Ask pupils to think about how someone who 'worshipped' each might behave.

- Give pupils pupils Post-it ® notes and ask them to fill in their ideas – and then to walk round and stick them up on the charts.

- Alternatively you could copy and give out the grid below for pupils to fill in their ideas.

- See bottom of page 9 for activities to follow on from this.

What does this person worship?		
	My suggestion	**A reason for my suggestion**
What might this person read?		
Where might this person like to go a lot?		
What would this person try to do?		
What might this person enjoy?		
What might this person celebrate?		
What difference might worship make to this person's life?		

© 2009 RE Today Services
Permission is granted to photocopy this page for use in classroom activities in schools that have purchased this publication.

5. An assessment activity

This simple fill-in sheet could be used by individual pupils, or tackled by pairs.

Using a framework like this (it could be simplified for younger children) enables teachers to assemble some evidence of what children in the primary years are learning and achieving in RE.

Name/s

1. This is a list of things we have thought of that money can't buy:

(a)

(b)

(c)

(d)

(e)

2. Here is a drawing of one thing that money cannot buy which we think is priceless:

6. From the work we've done in RE about worship and money, I have learned...

I have been thinking about...

3. The reason I've chosen this thing as a priceless object is....

The reason it is so valuable is because...

5. The Buddhist scriptures say 'The wise are generous: they go to a happier world.' What I think about this is...

4. The Christian Bible says 'the love of money is the start of all kinds of evil'. What I think about this is...

© 2009 RE Today Services
Permission is granted to photocopy this page for use in classroom activities in schools that have purchased this publication.

Exploring worship: a visual learning and discussion activity

For the teacher

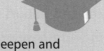

The activities in this section aim to deepen and broaden children's understanding of worship – what it is and how it is expressed.

The line drawing on pages 14–15 provides a visual stimulus to engage children in thinking about the rich variety that worship might mean. It includes such easily observable aspects as places 'where' people worship and artefacts which 'help' people to worship. But it also aims to take children further, to encourage them to think and talk about the 'what',' how' and 'why' aspects of worship, and to encourage them to recognise some non-religious contexts in which people may be said to be 'worshipping'!

The activities suggest some practical ways you might engage children in using and responding to the line drawing through thinking, speaking and reflecting. You will think of others.

I can …

The following pupil-friendly criteria could be used to assess children's responses to the activities. Level 4 describes what most 11-year-olds should be able to do.

Level 3

- use a developing religious vocabulary to describe some ways in which people worship (AT1)

- *ask thoughtful questions about how, why and what people worship today. (AT2)*

Level 4

- use a developing religious vocabulary to describe and show understanding of worship as an expression of devotion to that which matters most to people (AT1)

- *raise and suggest answers to questions and issues raised by worship. (AT2)*

Talk and respond activity outline

Photocopy the line drawing on pages 14–15 for children to share in pairs. Blank out the word 'Worship' for the starter below. Alternatively scan the image and display on the whiteboard.

- **Starter activity** (5–10 mins): Tell children that the artist has forgotten to put a title to this work – what do they think it might be? Feedback suggestions and reasons to the group.

- **Session 1 Paired activity:** Give each pair one card from 1-5 below. Ask them to talk about and respond to the questions and activities shown and be ready to present their responses to the rest of the class.

- **Session 2** Sit pupils in **groups** according to the activity they did in the previous session (all who did card 1 together and so on). Appoint a group leader to chair and someone to keep a note of any ideas that are shared. Each pair shows and explains their poster to the others. Each group reports back to the whole class. Record key ideas on the whiteboard.

Focus question: *Why do people worship?*

- Give each group a sheet of paper with this question at the centre. Ask children to record their ideas. The interviews with children from pages 16–33 could be used to support this activity. Gather responses.

- Explain that for many, religious worship is an outward expression of devotion to God. Many people find that worship helps them discover 'spiritual treasure' such as courage, faith, hope and love.

- **Reflection:** Give children a sheet of paper with a 'treasure chest' at the centre and the words *'The treasure in my life…'* Ask children to express in words, and pictures their ideas of 'treasures' in their lives that money cannot buy.

RE Today weblink:

A full colour version of the drawing on pages 14–15 is available for download by subscribers from the RE Today website. Go to www.retoday.org.uk Enter the password found in your termly RE Today magazine) and click on curriculum resources.

Talk and respond cards for group activity

1. Where do people worship?

- From the picture, find and make a list of the different places where believers show their devotion to God. Remember, this is not always in a special building.

- Use your ideas to make a poster to show others about WHERE PEOPLE WORSHIP. Include pictures, words and colours.

- Write a short report (no more than 150 words) to explain what you have included in your poster and why.

2. When do people worship?

- From the picture find out what you can about times, days and seasons when believers show their devotion to God.

- Use your ideas to make a poster to show others about WHEN PEOPLE WORSHIP. Include pictures, words and colours.

- Write a short report (no more than 150 words) to explain what you have included in your poster and why.

3. How do people worship?

- From the picture, find and list as many different ways as you can of how religious believers show their devotion to God. Compare your list with a partner and tick any you have both chosen.

- Use your ideas to make a poster to show others about HOW PEOPLE WORSHIP. Include pictures, words and colours to show the feelings of worship.

- Write a short report (no more than 150 words) to explain what you have included in your poster and why.

4. What things help people to worship?

- From the picture, pick out anything you think would help someone to think about and remember God. It might be an object, a book, a place, a person.

- Use your ideas to make a poster to show others about THINGS THAT HELP PEOPLE WORSHIP. Include pictures, words and colours.

- Write a short report (no more than 150 words) to explain what you have included in your poster and why.

5. Who or what do people worship today?

- People 'worship' lots of different things. **What matters most to you is what you worship.** Look at the picture and use your own ideas to make a list of things that 'matter most' to people today.

- Use your ideas to make a poster to show others about WHO AND WHAT PEOPLE WORSHIP TODAY. Include pictures, words and colours.

- Write a short report (no more than 150 words) to explain what you have included in your poster and why.

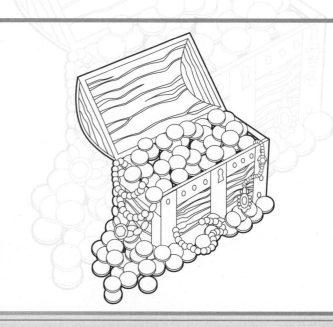

© 2009 RE Today Services
Permission is granted to photocopy this page for use in classroom activities in schools that have purchased this publication.

© 2009 RE Today Services Illustrated by Sophie Hardwicke

Worship & Devotion

When?

How?

Why?

Fajr Zuhr Asr Magrib Isha

✝ St John's Church Notices ✝

Daily Services
Monday to Friday 10am
Evensong 7:30pm

Sunday Services
Communion & Sermon 10am

Prayer Group Tonight
7pm
at the Cottage

Bible Study
Wednesday 6pm

October

THANK YOU!
WE RAISED
⭐ £235 ⭐
AT OUR CAR BOOT
⭐ SALE TO HELP ⭐
HOMELESS PEOPLE
⭐ ⭐ ⭐

Hope Goodness Devotion Love
Self Control
Comfort Joy Faithfulness
Kindness Peace thanksgiving
Forgiveness

© 2009 RE Today Services Illustrated by Sophie Hardwicke
Permission is granted to photocopy this page for use in classroom activities in schools that have purchased this publication.

Meeting young worshippers

7-11

Meet Chloe: a Roman Catholic Christian

Chloe is 9 and lives with her parents and older brothers in Hereford. The family are Roman Catholic Christians.

What does worship mean to you and your family?

The gospel stories are very important to me and I like to think about how the disciples worshipped and followed Jesus. One of the most important times in the **Mass** in church (we go every Sunday) is the reading of the **Gospel**. We must listen very carefully to the story. When I am not **serving on the altar** during mass, I like going out to the Children's Liturgy. I enjoy playing instruments when we sing the **Gloria**. I worship at home, when I say my prayers. My Dad always reminds me to say my prayers every night. There is a prayer I learned a long time ago that I say every night, and I say the **Our Father** and the **Hail Mary**. When I say my prayers in my bedroom I like to look at a statue of **Mary** and **Jesus** that I got for my **First Holy Communion**. I like to polish the statue.

How does worship make you feel?

I am an **altar server** and it is a special job. It gives me a swirly feeling inside – nervous but proud. I have to wear a special robe. I carry a candle in the procession. When I am older, I will carry the cross. I am in front of all the congregation helping Father Nicholas to prepare the **bread and wine** for the mass. The bread and wine is important because in the Gospel story, on the night before Jesus died, he took bread and broke it and said 'Take this all of you and eat it. This is my body which is given up for you.' That is how Father blesses the bread and then I have to **ring the bell** to show that it is a very special moment, when everyone is praying. I have to put the bell down again very carefully. Then Father blesses the wine and I ring the bell again. As altar servers, we are first to receive communion, then the congregation.

If you could pick one special item/symbol/object to represent worship for you, what would it be and why?

I would probably say a candle, because when I pray – at school and at church – when I am carrying the candle as an altar server, instead of closing my eyes I look at the candle really really deeply and I can see Jesus. I remember that Jesus is the light of the world and that is not going to change.

Where for you is your most 'spiritual' place?

I would say in the church on the altar, close to the **tabernacle** (where the bread and wine is held) because it is the closest place I can ever be to Jesus and God. We believe Jesus is really there in the bread and wine. When I go to the side after my communion I can pray quietly near all the lovely candles.

© 2009 RE Today Services
Permission is granted to photocopy this page for use in classroom activities in schools that have purchased this publication.

Exploring Christian Eucharist

For the teacher

The interview with Chloe provides a good 'way in' for pupils to start thinking deeply about the Eucharist. Eucharist comes from a Greek word meaning 'thanksgiving'. It is the word used by most Christians to describe the sacred meal in which they take part. It has many other names. Each one emphasises a part of the worship: The Lord's Supper; The Breaking of the Bread; The Holy Communion; The Mass. Mass is chiefly used in Roman Catholic churches.

Activity 1 The story of the Last Supper

- Look at some images of the Last Supper. Read/tell the story of the Last Supper (Luke ch 22, v 14-23).

- Act out the story, taking digital photos of key moments. Put photos into a whiteboard flipchart or comic strip format with blank speech and thought bubbles.

- Children write in speech and thought bubbles over the photos what they think the disciples were saying and thinking at points during the story.

- Why do the children think Jesus set up the celebration of the sharing of bread and wine for the Early Church?

Activity 3 Exploring First Communion

- **Watch** a video clip or PowerPoint presentation showing a child's first communion. As they watch, ask children to note down at least one 'big' question they want to ask. Such 'big' questions often start with 'Why?

- In small groups children **share questions**. Identify 2–3 key questions. Groups feedback questions. As a class, identify up to six big questions which can be put to a Christian visitor. Talk about what answers they think a Christian like Chloe might give to these questions.

- **Invite a Christian** (or, ideally, two Christians from different traditions) to come and answer questions about how they feel about the Eucharist or Holy Communion. Children ask the key question they decided upon.

- In a follow-up session, decide what **similarities and differences** there are between the different denominations' approaches to the Eucharist.

Activity 2 What happens in the Eucharist?

Identify the five main sections of the Eucharist service: confession, forgiveness, remembrance, reflection and sharing. Create mind-maps of how these features of the communion service are evident in everyday life, for example:

- *Confession/forgiveness* – the value of saying sorry. What one thing would the pupils like to say sorry for? Children could write their responses secretly onto whiteboards and wipe off, or on bits of paper which are then ritually torn up. **Paired talk/shared feedback:** How does it feel to have something you are sorry for wiped away? Who are Christians like Chloe saying sorry to in the Eucharist?

- *Remembrance* – ways of remembering special people and times. **Paired talk shared feedback:** What special time can you remember and why? Who are Christians remembering in the Eucharist and why?

- *Reflection* – the value of quiet and stillness to provide a space in their lives. Experiment with a time of stilling or quiet meditation. **Paired talk/ shared feedback:** Ask pupils to talk about how silence makes them feel. How it helps. How might it help Chloe as she worships?

- *Sharing* – the value of special family celebrations/meals. If possible plan and share a simple class meal. **Paired talk/shared feedback:** Why did it feel special? Why do Christians share bread and wine at this special service?

See also

REQuest : www. request.org.uk/

Christianity Unpacked: a free 3-CD set containing a PowerPoint presentation on Communion in the section 'What's It Like To Be A Christian?'

BBC DVD Pathways of Belief: The Church – includes First Communion in a RC church.

www.youtube.co.uk includes many examples of children's First Communions.

Meet Rebekah and Sam: Anglicans (Church of England)

Sam (8) and Rebekah (10) live in Leicestershire with their mum and dad. They are members of Holy Trinity Church, which is an Anglican church.

What does worship mean to you and how does it make you feel?

Rebekah: Our church is in a big room with chairs for hundreds of people. There's a stage at the front, for the music groups who lead the worship. Sometimes my mum plays the clarinet. The church also has lots of little rooms for different children's groups. Every Sunday we worship all together for the first part of the service: we sing songs and there's time for the children, something interesting about the Bible. Once a month, we all have Holy Communion together. Our whole family goes to share bread and wine. I take the bread, but not the wine because it's alcoholic, and I'm a bit young. That's when I think about other people who need us to pray for them, perhaps when they are in trouble. My one word to describe church is 'exciting!'

Sam: I think about the story of Jesus, when he broke the bread and shared the wine with his disciples. He said that the bread stands for his body and the wine stands for his blood. What I like about our church is our Explorers group, for 7–10s, we make things a lot. Our leaders are really funny and we often do drama. One of our ministers, Bill, did a talk about the stained-glass window one Sunday. It shows why our church is called 'Holy Trinity Church', because it shows that God is three in one: God the father, Jesus and the Holy Spirit. When it is time to pray in church, I really like looking at the stained-glass windows. My one word to describe church would be 'Fun.'

Sam: 'I chose this cross because I think it's really good (it comes from Rwanda, in Africa). Someone has used a little twig to make the cross, and it's detailed. It's really good because Jesus hung on a wooden cross in the Easter story and this is Jesus, made out of wood.

If you could pick one object to represent worship for you, what would it be and why?

Rebekah: 'I chose this cross because it has got a Bible verse on it that I like. "Love always protects, always trusts, always hopes, always perseveres." The words from the Bible make it extra special.'

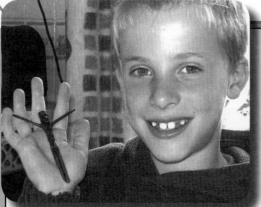

Where for you is your most 'spiritual' place?

Rebekah: Our Explorers group from church went on a weekend away together. We stayed in a chapel that has been converted to have dormitories. It was really fun. I like it that we learn the Bible in Explorers and at home. I love lots of Bible stories. We went to Wicksteed Park, and swimming, and we had fireworks. We had a great laugh. We had 'time for God' as well, and made 'thanksgiving flags'. I liked the 'God time' when we heard the story of a boy who gave up his lunch, for Jesus to feed the crowd. Our leader Jill had lots of stuff for us to use to make clay fish. It shows that Jesus can help people with anything.

Sam: My favourite part was making up verses to a song to sing of things to thank God for. My friend Jacob made up a verse thanking God for nature and someone else made up a verse about thanking God for tomato ketchup.

© 2009 RE Today Services
Permission is granted to photocopy this page for use in classroom activities in schools that have purchased this publication.

For the teacher

- Rebekah and Sam worship in a Church of England community. Use this interview to help your pupils to learn about aspects of Christian worship and community and think about their own lives and experiences.

- The church the children attend has its own website, which includes details of the group Sam and Rebekah are in, and lots of photos. Children might like to have a look: www.holytrinityleics.force9.co.uk

- The two children refer to the Bible several times. Good learning from these texts is a useful addition to this work. They include:
  - the Feeding of 5000 in Luke ch 9 vs 10-17
  - the Last Supper in Luke ch 22 vs 7-23
  - the Easter story, in Luke chs 23 and 24
  - St Paul's love poem from 1 Corinthians ch 13 vs 4-7.

Thanksgiving flags

The 'thanksgiving flags' that Rebekah refers to are shown above. Holy Trinity Explorers used them to create simple prayers of thanks to God, and 'planted' them in the garden of their hostel. They are easy to make with pieces of rainbow-coloured paper wrapped round a bamboo stick. In the plural school, children should have the choice: would you like to thank God, or someone else? What for?

Activity 1   What matters?

Give pupils this list of 12 words from the article, on the whiteboard or on paper. Ask them to choose from the list five things that matter to Sam and five for Rebekah, and say why. Then choose five things that are important to them and say why. What are the similarities and differences they notice?

Friends	Tomato ketchup	Praying
Music	Family	Love
Drama	Church	Wicksteed Park
Bible	Bread	Wine
God	Fun	Worship

Activity 2 Sam and Rebekah: what are they like?

Write a short description of Sam or Rebekah, using all the information from the interview, and their photos. Include your description of their religion.

Activity 3 What does the Bible say about love?

Read 1 Corinthians ch 13 vs 4-7 with the class. Discuss the words Rebekah uses, and all the other ideas about love in the Bible passage. This part of the Bible is often read at weddings. Consider why, and think about why it is often read at funerals too.

Activity 4 Making 'thanksgiving flags'

Ask pupils to think about what Christians thank God for. Listen together to a piece of Christian music that gives thanks to God. Ask pupils about saying thank you, and why it is important, and give them time, while listening to the music, to create a flag of thanks for themselves – thanking God, or someone else to whom they are grateful.

Meet Rachel: a Pentecostal Christian

Rachel is 10 and lives with her mum, dad and two 'annoying' brothers in Coulsdon, outer London. They are Pentecostal Christians.

What does worship mean to you and your family?

My family and I like going to **church** together to **worship** God. I like talking to God and singing, sharing with my friends at church and talking to them.

I also go to Kings Club, which is like Sunday school. It is a special time during the service for children to go out and learn more about God in a fun way. We often play games and one of my favourites is learning the memory verse from the **Bible**.

Worship is about listening as well. In Kings Club we sit on mats on the floor and listen to what God is saying to us individually and we write it down. God told me once that 'though things may be rough, you will get through it'. I was very shocked and excited to hear God speak to me. It encouraged me more and made me realise that God does listen to my prayers and will help me. It makes me want to go on with him.

Sometimes in the service adults will share what God has told them with everyone, or they will **speak in tongues**. I like hearing people speak in tongues in the worship, but I can't do that yet, it's a language which God gives them to praise him.

How does worship make you feel?

I think worship is fun! Worshipping and **praising** God makes me feel very happy and joyful. It makes me feel that I am special.

At our church we have a band and some singers who help us to worship with singing. **The best part of the worship for me is being able to move my hands and feet, clap and dance to the music.** The music has a good beat and some people wave banners and dance. Sometimes the words to a song touch me. I like the slow songs too because they make me think hard about God.

If you could pick one special item/ symbol/ object to represent worship for you – what would it be and why?

I think the **bread and wine** are very special. I like taking **communion,** it makes me feel part of God's family and important to him. My mum and dad have communion every week, but I only have it when it is a family service and everybody in our church gets together and talks about God.

In our church it is lovely, there are lots of different people from all over the world and I feel we are all part of a big family. It feels very good to share the bread and wine with them all–it's like having a big family party.

Where for you is your most 'spiritual' place?

For me church is the most spiritual place. I know I can talk to God at home but I find it easier to talk and listen to him at church. Listening to others share what God has done for them and how he has healed and helped people encourages me.

© 2009 RE Today Services
Permission is granted to photocopy this page for use in classroom activities in schools that have purchased this publication.

Exploring Christian worship

For the teacher

This interview captures the joy of worship and of belonging to a Christian church for this 10-year-old.

In pairs or small groups ask children to

- use the grid to identify and talk about some of the different ways in which Rachel worships God and how these make her feel.

- use a blank grid to create their own multi-sensory space for worship. What would they taste, touch, look at, listen to?

Talking and working together to explore Rachel's experiences and feelings **will enable children to**

- describe and show understanding of religious practices, feelings and experiences *(AT1 Level 4 in the English Non-Statutory Framework for RE)*

- describe why people belong to religions. *(AT1 Level 5)*

- Descibe what inspires and influences them. *(AT2 Level 4)*

For information

Speaking in tongues

When Jesus' apostles were filled with the Holy Spirit, Acts Ch 2 v 1-13 tells us that they spoke in languages they had not learnt. Pentecostal Christians believe the Holy Spirit still fills people and they praise God by speaking the words he gives them to say. This usually happens during a time of praise and worship.

Listening to God: Rachel tells us that she hears God speaking as a very strong feeling, sometimes it is a picture in her mind.

	What does Rachel do?	**How does this make her feel?**
Taste		
See		
Hear		
Touch		
Smell		

Meet Samuel: an Orthodox Jew

Samuel is 10 and lives in Ilford, Essex, with his mother and father. He is Orthodox Jewish.

What does worship mean to you?

I use the word **prayer**. Worship sounds like worshipping idols, which is not in the Jewish religion. When I pray, I thank **Hashem** for all things we have, like food, being healthy and having enough money to survive in good surroundings.

When I pray, it is a double prayer, saying and thinking. I speak the prayer for people I know the most, my family and my friends. I also think inside about everyone I don't know, the other people in the world, and hope they will be in a safe environment.

How does prayer make you feel?

In **synagogue**, I like hearing the prayers for the sick and listening to who is included in them. When the rabbi says their names, I picture them in my mind and think of them getting better.

On **Shabbat** I am sometimes asked to sing a special hymn praising Hashem in synagogue, it is called the Hymn of Glory. Sometimes I am tired when I do it because I have stayed up late for Friday night meal, but I would never refuse. It is a **mitzvah**, something you do selflessly for the benefit of other people. You don't just do it for yourself. When the **Torah** comes round, I get my **tsitsit** out, kiss the fringes and kiss the Torah. You also get the kiss of the Torah back, because when you do it more holiness comes to you.

If you could pick one object to represent worship for you, what would it be and why?

The **Havdalah** candle
I like to think Hashem is in the flame watching us, and when the candle is out, he has gone back to heaven and taken bad things away, like **loshon hora** (speaking badly about people behind their backs), murder, kidnapping, and bullying. The candle is twisted. All good things are twirled round with the pattern, good things like **mitzvot**, being nice to people, helping Mum cook without being asked. You can feel Hashem's presence in the flickering, the warmth is like him embracing you.

Where for you is your most spiritual place?

When I am standing on the **bimah**, singing and when I see the Torah when the ark is opened. I feel Hashem is nearer to me. When the **ark** is shut, it feels like a barrier. I think I would feel close to God on a hill, or on the top of a mountain. There would be no one to interfere, no TV to bring news of bad things, like another missing person. I wouldn't see anything disturbing. I could look at the whole world. As I would be higher up, I would feel nearer to him.

© 2009 RE Today Services

For the teacher

It is important to note that both Jewish children interviewed (see interview with Michelle, next page) did not use the word 'worship' and that Sam felt uncomfortable with the word. This shows that some terms in religions do not reach across all faiths.

Sam's reflective view of his Jewish faith shows how he interprets his religious actions. He talks happily about the inside and outside world of prayer. He has a very personal reading of the meaning of the Havdalah candle and how he responds to the Torah during its procession. These are readings that are not traditionally seen in RE books about Judaism, but which are more connected with the Chassidic tradition of spirituality.

As with Michelle, the practical element of Judaism, shown in ethical actions, shines through in Sam's interview. He talks about doing mitzvot – good deeds or kind acts – and the importance of not speaking ill of others (loshon hora).

Sam's love for 'klal Israel' – the Jewish community of people – was in the forefront of his mind. Pupils could discuss the many examples in his interview which illustrate this, such as his concern for the sick and ill of the congregation.

Activity 1 Using music, talk and movement to express learning

- Pupils **listen to the song** 'When You Believe' (from *Prince of Egypt*). This can be downloaded from www.homeofhope.co.uk and the lyrics from http://homeofhope.co.uk/Documents/HomeofHope.pdf. **In pairs talk about:** What are the messages in the song? What questions come to the mind when you hear it?

- Pupils make two lists. One is everything that **Sam believes**, from the interview. The other is **what they believe**. It need not be religious beliefs, but could be views about the world, or how people should behave.

- Pupils then, in pairs or groups, **mime** examples of mitzvot (good deeds or kind acts), using examples from Sam's interview and their own ideas. These can be shown to the class, who have to guess the good deeds being shown.

- Each pair or group can then put their mimes together, using the background music of 'When You Believe' and **creating a dance or movement piece**.

Activity 2 Using an artefact and collage to express insights

- Pupils watch a plaited Havdalah candle being lit and reflect on how they feel. They quietly write down words or phrases that come into their mind as they see it burning. They then see the candle extinguished into a saucer or bowl of water. They write down the words or phrases that come into their mind. How do their reflections compare with Sam's thoughts?

- Using examples cut from newspapers and magazines, pupils make two collages that show Sam's personal interpretation of the Havdalah candle. One poster will show the Havdalah candle alight, with pictures of the positive things Sam has mentioned, including the mitzvot. The other will show the candle when it is out, with images that suggest darkness, endings and loss.

Meet Michelle

Michelle is 13 and lives in Ilford, Essex with her parents and sister Sarah, aged 11. Michelle's parents belong to a Reform Jewish synagogue and her grandparents go to the Orthodox Jewish synagogue, so she goes to both.

What does worship mean to you?

I say the word 'praying' and not worship. I pray for my family to be healthy and not to have any illnesses that cause them to go into hospital. In my prayers I say thank you to **Hashem** for keeping my parents safe, for the food we have and for looking after me. I ask Hashem to keep the world peaceful and to help people who are poor.

I like praying at special times, like on **Shabbat**. I would miss Friday night **Kiddush**, the special prayers we say before we light the candles and eat.

I am going to have my **batmitzvah** this summer. I have to read from the **Torah** in Hebrew, in front of everyone in **synagogue**. This is very hard for me as I have special needs but I am pushing myself. My parents help me when I struggle and get stuck on a word.

I think children who have special needs should try to do their **bar or batmitzvah**. My advice is, 'You are different but you also are the same as everyone else. Try your best, the best you can. Always ask for help if you need it. Remember it is your special day and that you are special in your own way.'

How does praying make you feel?

Praying makes me happy and gives me a good feeling inside. I feel Jewish all the time. I pray in my head all through the day and in **synagogue**. When I pray inside, I ask Hashem to help me stop getting angry, to calm me down and to stop bad feelings. When I pray in **synagogue**, it feels powerful because you are praying with other people and saying the same prayers together. When I was with Grandma in **synagogue** on **Shabbat**, I saw a girl turn on her mobile phone during the service. I told her to switch it off. It is important to have respect for people who are praying and you also shouldn't carry things on **Shabbat**.

If you could pick one special item to represent worship for you what would it be and why?

My Star of David necklace: When I was little, Grandma and Grandpa bought me back a **kemaya** from Israel, a Star of David necklace. My cousins live in Israel and I would like to go to **Jerusalem** and see everyone praying at the Western Wall. I always wear my necklace when I go to synagogue, as well as my smart clothes, so it makes me think of **Shabbat** and praying. I go with my grandma to her synagogue and help her up the steps. It is the Jewish thing to do.

Where for you is your most spiritual place?

When I get angry, I always sit at the bottom of the stairs, being still. That place calms me down. But a special place I remember was the Isle of Wight. We went there on holiday. It was peaceful and calm. I liked the sand and listening to all the different sounds. I remember playing sandcastles with my sister.

© 2009 RE Today Services
Permission is granted to photocopy this page for use in classroom activities in schools that have purchased this publication.

For the teacher

- The Talmud says, 'Gadol k'vod habriyot' – 'great is the value of human dignity'. This theme runs through Michelle's interview. She sees her Jewish faith as not a collection of rules, but as something that guides her to lead a caring life and which helps her with her difficulties. Michelle found it hard to think of a spiritual place, probably because her Jewish identity is so strong. She identifies being Jewish as her family and community, rather than a location.

- The following activity aims to help pupils reflect on how a new Jewish place of worship might be designed to promote equality for all in line with the ethical thinking in Michelle's interview. It also links with her commitment to preparing for her bat mitzvah, despite her special needs.

- Preparation for this task could be to watch the movie trailer for the American film *Praying with Lior* www.prayingwithlior.com. This is about a boy with Downs Syndrome as he approaches his bar mitzvah. Pupils could be alerted that some of the language used to describe children with disabilities is different from the words we use in Britain. The film shows how inclusion benefits the whole Jewish community.

Role play activity: creating an inclusive synagogue

Using the following scenario, ask pupils to imagine that they are advisers to the committee members who have to make a decision about the design of a new synagogue.

In groups ask pupils to:

- decide on the order of priority that they feel Michelle would choose, explaining their reasons by giving examples from her interview.

- make a list of practical suggestions about how the new synagogue will solve the problems, and make some drawings to show design ideas

- make a presentation to the class to share ideas for the new Bet Shivyon synagogue.

In a plenary agree ideas that fit best with the inclusive spirit of Bet Shivyon and decide on a mission statement for the new synagogue that sums up its values. It could have this structure....

> Bet Shivyon – a Reform synagogue that aims to bring...............
> and create.................................
> in the spirit of..................

A Reform synagogue has raised money to have a new building.
It is going to be called 'Bet Shivyon' – *House of Equality*.
It is an opportunity to make a new start and show the importance of equality for all.
Members had a meeting and made these comments about the old synagogue, which is in a traditional building:

- It is difficult for people with physical disabilities to read from the Torah as the bimah has steps and the reading desk is too high for someone in a wheelchair.

- The Hebrew in the Torah is hard for people with visual impairment to read.

- Some of the Sunday religion school teachers, although kind, don't have experience of teaching children with special needs.

- All members of the congregation should meet together more often, whether they are able-bodied or disabled.

- More children with special needs should celebrate their bar or bat mitzvah in synagogue, including those who are deaf, visually impaired, or have speech and communication difficulties.

© 2009 RE Today Services
Permission is granted to photocopy this page for use in classroom activities in schools that have purchased this publication.

Meet Nia: a Hindu

Nia is 9 years old and lives with her parents, sister Maya and brother Raj in Coventry. She and her family are Hindu.

What does worship mean to you?

To me worship means time to get away from everyone and to sit in peace and relax. It also means lighting a **diva** (holy flame) and sitting in front of an image of God praying for everyone's happiness and good health. I also ask God for blessings so that I become a better person as I get older. If I could not worship I would miss being able to light the diva and having that quiet time. I would also miss going to the **mandir** (temple) where I can sit and listen to the **arti** (worship song) and **bhajans** (hymns).

How does worship make you feel?

When I'm praying I feel very **spiritual**. I also feel very calm, relaxed and happy, knowing that I'm doing something I enjoy. I feel extremely proud to be a Hindu and to be able to take part in lots of religious festivals and ceremonies.

If you could pick one object to represent worship, for you, what would it be and why?

There are many special items, symbols and objects which represent worship, but **my** special item is a diva. This is because we light a diva for all occasions and ceremonies, whether happy or sad, at any time and in any size, from one small flame to hundreds all lit at once! I also like the diva as it lights up everything.

Where for you is your most spiritual place?

For me the most spiritual place has to be jointly the **mandir room** at home, where I can pray alone and where we worship together as a family, and also the Shree Krishna Mandir in Coventry.

I feel totally at peace there as no one is allowed to talk during prayer times and there is complete silence. I can think about things and not be disturbed. There are big, beautiful statues of gods and goddesses and bells to ring. After prayers, the priest gives you some **prashad** – which is food (usually dried fruit, nuts and sweets) that has been offered before God in thanks and we believe is blessed by God.

 © 2009 RE Today Services
Permission is granted to photocopy this page for use in classroom activities in schools that have purchased this publication.

Meet Saksham: a Hindu

Saksham is 11 years old and lives with his parents and brother Dhruv in Wrexham. He and his family are Hindu.

What does worship mean to you?

Worship to me means a way of getting closer to God. To wish for something you really want and to confess all your sins and crimes. It's something that makes my family feel close.

How does worship make you feel?

It makes me feel very relaxed and very happy from the inside. I think it's a good way of communicating with and getting your feelings across to God and to other people. I usually worship with my family, but there isn't a Hindu community in Wrexham, only a few Hindu people. I have different feelings when I worship just with my family and when we are part of a large group worshipping together. I can be more open when I'm with my family but it's also great with more people as you feel part of a group and proud to be there.

If you could pick one object to represent worship for you, what would it be and why?

My special symbol would be the **Aum** (drawn too), mainly because it's the symbol for the Hindu religion, so I feel it's my symbol. It also means a lot to me as it represents God. I worship God **as** the Aum symbol **and** by using the Aum symbol.

Where for you is your most spiritual place?

My most spiritual place is a temple because it's a special place of worship for Hindus. However there isn't a Hindu temple in Wrexham, so living here means I also feel the **shrine** (place set aside for worship) in our kitchen at home is also a very spiritual place for me.

Every evening at about 7 o'clock, we all gather at the shrine to worship and pray as a family. There are big pictures of different gods and goddesses, such as **Durga** who is a goddess who sits on a tiger to show how powerful she is, and **Ganesh**, who has an elephant head and is believed to be very wise, which I like to look at. This is a peaceful and special time in the day.

© 2009 RE Today Services
Permission is granted to photocopy this page for use in classroom activities in schools that have purchased this publication.

For the teacher

The interviews with Nia and Saksham provide an excellent 'way in' to help pupils think deeply about what it means to belong to a group or community and about ways to connect with the divine.

The activities suggested here are designed to engage pupils in self-reflection and enquiry into what 'makes others tick' as well as broadening their knowledge and understanding of Hinduism.

Activity 1 Reflective activity

- Light a candle during circle time and ask pupils simply to gaze at the flame and think quiet thoughts.

- Follow up with paired, group or written feedback about how the flame makes them feel and what they associate with a flame. (Safe, afraid, warm? Memories of birthdays or special times?)

- Remind pupils about what Nia said about the use of diva lamps. Ask them to think about all the occasions when they might light a diva or a candle.

- In pairs, list as many as possible and share ideas in groups.

- Pupils then choose one occasion they feel is very special and detail it using pictures, words and perhaps even music if they wish. Some could be presented to the class or make a display.

Activity 2 Using artwork or presentation to show understanding of key terminology

In groups, pupils work together to produce posters that explain the meanings of diva, arti, bhajan and mandir.

(a) **Research** using carefully selected websites such as www.hindunet.org

(b) **Artwork** such as a large diva, arti tray, Indian instruments, mandir outline or pictures of gods or goddesses, could be done using paint, collage work, tissue paper, glitter and fabric.

(c) **Explanations** decided upon in groups and added to posters.

Alternatively, after step (a) pupils could choose to prepare a presentation on each item, perhaps with performance too.

Activity 3 Making music

Pupils compose their own hymn that praises creation or creator; group work to add musical accompaniment to some of the compositions; followed by performance.

Activity 4 Aum explored

Aum signifies the Hindu belief that God is all that there ever was, is and will be – pupils could try to produce their own symbol for eternity.

And/or research the many meanings of Aum, using carefully selected websites, and produce a PowerPoint or posters with a huge Aum in the centre surrounded by explanation of meanings.

Activity 5 A Hindu home shrine explored

Prepare an area of the classroom as a home shrine. A table draped with rich silk or cotton cloths in a corner would provide an appropriate setting.

Gather children around the shrine and read what Nia and Saksham say about this 'special place'. Allow a moment for their own quiet reflection

Pupils can complete all or any of following:

(a) List what you saw, smelt, heard, felt.

(b) Draw a home shrine and label it.

(c) Using cards provided, match items in the shrine or puja tray to their meaning.

(d) Personal reflection: If you had a family shrine what ideas of God would you have in there and why?

Remind pupils that Hindu gods and goddesses are visual representations of the innumerable facets and talents that make up the one God. Offer pupils the option of having symbols or objects rather than deities or people on their own 'shrine' and also include the option for those of no belief in the divine to reflect on who or what do you/would you worship and why? (Link to activities on pages 8–11.)

Objects found on a home shrine

Many different objects are found on a home shrine include pictures of the gods and goddesses and sometime a picture of a deceased loved one.

The items used in puja are:

• A small lamp (usually a dish with a cotton wool wick placed in vegetable oil or clarified butter)

• A small bell

• Freshly picked flowers or leaves

• Freshly drawn water, ideally in an iron or copper vessel

• Incense burning in a holder

• Red kum-kum powder or turmeric powder or sandalwood paste (for making the Tilak mark on the worshippers forehead.

• Offerings of Indian sweets, (fudge is a good alternative) or fresh fruit.

What can you see in this Hindu shrine?

© 2009 RE Today Services
Permission is granted to photocopy this page for use in classroom activities in schools that have purchased this publication.

Meet Fatima: a Shia Muslim

Fatima is 11 and lives in Bradford with her parents, brother and sister. She is a Shia Muslim.

Madinah: Fatimah's most 'spiritual' place

What does worship mean to you?

Worship is the reason we live on earth. Everything I do is all to do with worship. From the moment I wake up I worship Allah. I say a prayer when getting dressed, when I go into the bathroom, and when I walk to school too. Worship is praying, salat, five times a day, but being a good honest person is worship too.

I help my mother a lot because the Prophet Muhammad ﷺ said: 'Paradise lies at the feet of mothers.' I try not to tell lies and try to stop my classmates from bullying and also to be kind to all Allah's creatures like spiders and birds.

I also help my father in the mosque. When there is a special event I help him with the food and my special job is to work out all the bills and to write up what we are going to need. My dad says that I'm really good at budgeting so when I grow up he's going to make me the mosque's accountant!

If you could pick one special item to represent worship for you what would it be and why?

The Qur'an

My copy of the Qur'an represents worship for me.

The Qur'an tells us how we should worship Allah. It also tells us about Allah so that we know who we are worshipping.

My Qur'an is also translated into English which helps me understand what I'm reading. I keep my Qur'an at home. It was a special present from my father, which he bought for me in Madinah.

How does worship make you feel?

It makes me feel complete. It is the best thing in the world! It makes me forget my worries as soon as I stand on my prayer mat. I often pray with my Aunty and I feel like I'm under Allah's protection when I pray.

If I couldn't worship I would feel very unhappy. I'm so happy that I pray as it's why I have been sent here by God.

Where for you is your most 'spiritual place'?

Last year I went to Madinah and visited the Prophet Muhammad's mosque. It was the greatest moment of my life. I felt really special to have been selected by Allah to go there.

I went as close to the tomb of the Prophet ﷺ as I could. Then we all went to the Jannat al-Baqi, the cemetery where the Prophet's family is buried. I prayed a lot there and I cried so many tears when I remembered Prophet Muhammad ﷺ and his family.

At the Jannat al-Baqi we met Muslims from all over the world. Some of them spoke languages that we couldn't speak but we made friends there which I will cherish for ever.

© 2009 RE Today Services
Permission is granted to photocopy this page for use in classroom activities in schools that have purchased this publication.

For the teacher

These interviews with Fatima and Harris provide an excellent 'way in' for children to develop their understanding of the way in which religious belief impacts on day-to-day activity as well as the individual's hopes for the future (the afterlife).

Both are able to make clear connections between key people, events and places in the history of Islam, and their own lives many centuries later in 21st-century Yorkshire.

They also speak powerfully of their personal experience of worship and prayer, showing an understanding of its importance and meaning based on the teaching of the Qur'an as well as its impact on their own lives and spiritual well-being.

Activity 1 Spiritual photos

Spiritual Photos (www.spiritualphotos.com) is a large web-based collection of images on religious and spiritual themes.

Ask pupils to:

- **choose** 'Islam' in the 'World Religions & Spirituality' section and identify 10 images which they think would appeal to Fatima and Harris. What reasons can they give for their choice?

- **suggest** 'what's missing' from the collection of images of Islam. What new images would they like to add to the collection, and why?

- **take their own 'spiritual photo'** to express some of their own questions about religion and spirituality, and provide a caption and text for it.

Note: The site's copyright statement covers most classroom uses of the images – but do check.

Activity 2 Music

Nasheeds are Islam-oriented songs which are increasingly popular with young Muslims in the UK.

The **themes and lyrics** reflect and explore key beliefs and teachings in Islam: for example, prayer, worship, Prophet Muhammad ﷺ, Iman (faith), Ramadan.

Nasheeds are traditionally sung **a cappella**, and may be accompanied by a drum. This simple musical style is used because many Muslim scholars believe that Islam prohibits the use of musical instruments apart from some basic percussion to accompany the human voice.

Nasheeds are readily available on CD, and several are available from RE Today (see: www.retoday.org.uk). Popular contemporary singers include Zain Bhikka and Dawud Wharnsby Ali.

Ask pupils to:

- **listen** to some nasheeds by well-known Muslim musicians, e.g. 'Salaat' or 'It's Time to Pray' by Zain Bhikka on *Children of Heaven* or 'Praise to the Prophet' by Zain Bhikka on *Towards the Light* (both CDs available from RE Today).

- **identify** differences between the nasheeds and their own choice of music e.g.

  o simplicity of style

  o no instruments

  o religious themes in the lyrics.

- **suggest** how and why Harris and Fatima might find songs like this helpful.

- consider the following quote from Imam Al Ghazali – and suggest their own idea of the 'purpose of songs'

  'The purpose of songs is to inspire the spirit to love Allah and the song which can inspire the listener to the love of Allah is the real song'.

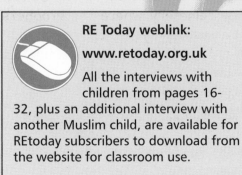

RE Today weblink:

www.retoday.org.uk

All the interviews with children from pages 16-32, plus an additional interview with another Muslim child, are available for REtoday subscribers to download from the website for classroom use.

Meet Harris: a Sunni Muslim

Harris is 11 and lives in Wakefield with his family.
He is a Sunni Muslim.

What does worship mean to you?

Worship means a lot to me. In Arabic it is
called **Ibadah** (I worship the One God). We
call God 'Allah'. Allah is One and Unique. He
doesn't have any sons or daughters and he is
our Creator. I worship him to thank him for
everything He has done for me and my family.

When I pray I turn towards Makkah and I
concentrate on what I am praying. I make
sure that there is nothing to distract me like
the TV or any other sounds. It's good to pray
in a quiet place.

If I couldn't worship then I would miss most
of all praying five times a day! If we didn't
worship then we would be sinning. We have
been created to worship Allah and that's the
most important thing to do.

How does worship make you feel?

Worship makes me feel so good inside! It
makes me feel relaxed whevever I perform
the namaz. The namaz is a name given to the
prayers Muslims say five times a day.

If I pray five times a day my sins will be
forgiven and I will, Insha'Allah (God willing), go
to Jannat. Jannat is our name for heaven. In
Jannat you can have whatever you want.

If I miss a prayer I feel terrible. I feel guilty
inside, so I try not to miss my prayers.

If you could pick one special item to represent worship for you, what would it be and why?

The **musallah** (prayer mat)

My musallah, or prayer mat, is very
important to me. I use it to pray on
whenever I need to pray. It is clean and
I take my shoes off before standing on
it. My family each have their own prayer
mats.

If you do not use a prayer mat to
pray then it's not good, as you might
be praying on a place that hasn't been
cleaned. For the same reason we also
take our shoes off before going to the
mosque and as we come into our homes.

Where for you is your most 'spiritual place'?

My special place is the Ka'bah because it is the main holy
place for Muslims all over the world. Wherever they may be,
this is the place everyone turns to.

When people have been to the Ka'bah, they return as
special people and their name changes. They are called
'Hajji' if they are male or 'Hajjah' if they are female. I know
many Hajjis.

Hajjis bring special zamzam water from a well near the
Ka'bah. They also bring dates and gifts with them too! One
day, Insha'Allah (God willing), I will go to the Ka'bah too.

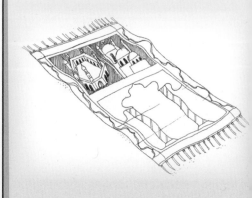

© 2009 RE Today Services
Permission is granted to photocopy this page for use in classroom activities in schools that have purchased this publication.